THE SAINT AUGUSTINE LECTURE SERIES

Villanova University
Augustinian Institute

Saint Augustine and the Augustinian Tradition

EDITOR

Russell J. DeSimone, O.S.A.

ASSOCIATE EDITORS

Benedict A. Paparella, Ph.D.
John M. Quinn, O.S.A.

Copyright © 1989 by
Villanova University Press
All rights reserved

Library of Congress Catalog Card Number: 89-50151
ISBN 87723-050-1

THE SAINT AUGUSTINE LECTURE 1986

SAINT AUGUSTINE AND THE WESTERN TRADITION OF SELF-KNOWING

Edward Booth, O.P.

CONTENTS

SAINT AUGUSTINE AND THE WESTERN TRADITION OF SELF-KNOWING

ST. AUGUSTINE AND THE WESTERN TRADITION OF SELF-KNOWING

Matters of fact are matters of opinion: so, according to the view of Plato.[1]

The paradox can be expressed in other ways. 'What is present' to us, and which we know as familiar, has been taken, ontologically, in different ways: 'as the Ἕν, the unifying single One, as the Λόγος, the protective assembling together of the All, as the ἰδέα, οὐσία, ἐνέργεια, substantia, actualitas, perceptio, monad, as objectivity, as the posited quality in self-positing in the sense of the will of reason, of love, of power, as the will to will in the endless return of like (to like)': so, according to Martin Heidegger,[2] who comments that 'The unfolding of being's full capacity for change looks first of all like a history of being. But being has no history . . . . '[3]

In the discouraging presence of numerous conflicting ontologies, Heidegger's search for authentic being both kept the question open for being in general, and asserted the

---

1. The epithet was gratefully received from the late Fr. Quentin Johnston, O.P. (cf. *Republic*, 476C-480A.)

2. *Zur Sache des Denkens*, 2nd edn. (Tübingen, 1976), p. 7: 'Indessen können wir die Wandlungsfülle des Anwesens auch historisch feststellen durch den Hinweis, dass Anwesen sich zeigt als das Ἕν, das einigende einzig Eine, als der Λόγος, die das All verwahrende Versammlung, als die ἰδέα, οὐσία, ἐνέργεια, substantia, actualitas, perceptio, Monade, als Gegenstandlichkeit, als Gesetzkeit des Sichsetzens im Sinne des Willens der Vernunft, der Liebe, des Geistes, der Macht, als Wille zum Willen in der ewigen Wiederkehr des Gleichen.'

3. *Ib.*, pp. 7-8: 'Die Entfaltung der Wandlungsfülle des Seins sieht zunächst aus wie eine Geschichte des Seins. Aber das Sein hat keine Geschichte.'

self's pre-ontological awareness of being. The self as *Dasein*[4], which, 'thrown' into existence, alive and thinking, a subject of care, a subject to anxiety and confronted by death, can vouch for its own being and for other-being, notably in its understanding itself. 'Without (my having) any ontological perspicuity, it has become apparent that I myself am the being that we call *Dasein*, that is in the sense of able to be, for whom it is a matter to be this being. Though lacking ontological determinateness, *Dasein* understands itself as being-in-the-world. . . . it is not only (something) present at hand, but already has *itself*'.[5] Without ostentation, Heidegger has here merged the two themes which have claimed a priority in metaphysical reflection, by reason of their fundamentality: being and self-knowing.

For those who come to being indirectly from formal ontology there is a preliminary task of sifting the real content from out of ontological analyses; but whether one approaches being indirectly or directly, there is for everyone

4. The word is not a creation of Heidegger; as found in Kant and Hegel it can be translated as 'existence', or 'something existent'. But he uses it to signify a human consciousness, aware of being in himself and around him. The history (from Wolff onwards) is given in art. 'Dasein', by U. Wienbruch, in *Historisches Wörterbuch der Philosophie*, ed. J. Ritter, vol. 2, (Basel-Stuttgart, 1972), coll. 15-22.

5. *Sein und Zeit*, 15th edn. (Tübingen, 1979), p. 313: 'Ohne jede ontologische Durchsichtigkeit enthüllt es doch: das Seiende, das wir Dasein nennen, bin ich je selbst und zwar als Seinskönnen, dem es darum geht, dieses Seinde zu sein. Das Dasein versteht sich, obgleich ohne zureichende ontologische Bestimmtheit, als In-der-Weltsein. . . . es ist nicht nur vorhanden, sondern hat *sich*.' The translation is not of Macquarrie and Robinson.

the task of disciplined discernment.[6] This discernment leads to an acceptance that normally being cannot be thought of as it is for long periods. Self-knowing also demands discipline; but the self to which it has an easier access than to being is less likely to be concealed in a categorial structure. The self which is known to the self — which is also being — retains its original vitality; and because of the coincidence of self as knowing with self as known, this produces a reference point more tractable than being. And it can communicate this vitality and certainty to renew ontology itself.[7]

Mind has a constitutional need to coincide with itself, which it does in self-knowing. This is true whether it is considered in a state without regard to time, and actually coinciding with itself, or whether it is considered as developing through time towards a condition of coinciding with itself. To coincide with oneself in one's feelings is to experience satisfaction; not to coincide with oneself in one's feelings is to experience pain. The quality of mind is much finer, and

6. For St. Thomas, metaphysics used 'separatio' rather than 'abstractio': *Expositio super Librum Boethii de Trinitate*, q.5, art. 3, corp.

7. Husserl, for example, felt a 'crisis' in which the modern age turned from pride to 'a growing dissatisfaction' and distress. 'Want has invaded all the sciences, most recently as a want of method.' Hence, he thought, the value of transcendental phenomenology: 'It was this that overcame naturalistic objectivism . . . in the only possible way, by beginning one's philosophizing from one's own ego; and that purely as the author of all one accepts, becoming in this regard a purely theoretical spectator.' *Die Krisis des Europäischen Menschentums und die Philosophie, Husserliana*, 6, (The Hague, 1954), pp. 342, 346. Transl. by Q. Lauer as 'Philosophy and the Crisis of European Man', in *Phenomenology and the Crisis of Philosophy*, (New York, 1965); v. pp. 185, 190.

its activity more intense. We see in Aristotle, the neo-Platonists and St. Augustine, and the German 'idealists'[8], an examination of mind, either enjoying, or looking for, the self-equality which is natural to it. Consequently, we could also pursue an attendant theme, the situation of mind not coinciding with itself, not knowing itself: that is, alienated from itself.

The history of this tradition is discontinuous but recurrent, and in general uneven.[9] It arose in a pagan setting, where it corresponded to a recurrent Old Testament theme, and from both it passed into Christian tradition. Here its utilisation in conceptions of the Trinity has been particularly fruitful. Self-knowing arises with Plato and the Stoics as a condition of moral virtue; it occurs in Augustine[10] and

---

8. (Note that Kant described himself as a 'transcendental idealist': *Kritik der reinen Vernunft*, A (first edn.) p. 370, p. 491 (= B (second edn.) p. 519, as well as being an 'empirical realist', A p. 370.) With Hegel more than equality is looked for: like everything else, mind as truly mind is 'reflected into itself' (in sich selbst reflektiert), *Jenaer Systementwurfe* II, *Metaphysik*, ed. R.-P. Horstmann, Philosophische Bibliothek, 332 (Hamburg, 1982), pp. 137-9, espec. 139[6-8]. It is 'in-and-for-itself': cf. *Phänomenologie des Geistes*, *Sämtliche Werke, Jubiläumsausgabe* (= *SW*), ed. H. Glockner, (Stuttgart, 1927-40, with later facsimile edns.), vol. 2, p. 28: 'Dies Anundfürsichsein . . . ist die geistige Substanz'.

9. Many texts up to the twelfth century are brought together in vol. 1 of P. Courcelle, *Connais-toi toi-même, de Socrate à saint Bernard*, 3 vols. (Paris, 1974-5); vols. 2 and 3 contrast platonist and christian views.

10. *Vide, de Beata Vita*, 2,7; *Soliloquium*, II 1,1; *de Vera Religione*, 39,73; *de Trinitate*, XV 12,21; *de Civitate Dei*, XI 26. cf. E. Booth, ('St. Augustine's "notitia sui" related to Aristotle and the Early neo-Platonists' (published in *Augustinianum*, I: 27 (1977), pp. 70-104; II: ib., pp. 104-132; III ib., pp. 364-401; IV: 28 (1978), pp. 183-221; V: 29 (1979), pp. 97-124), I, pp. 91-2, n. 74.

Descartes[11] in the form of the *cogito*: that the sureness of oneself in the act of thinking or doubting is a certainty unpregnable to doubt. But we shall exclude these two aspects, and consider self-knowing, or self-thinking, as it appears first in Aristotle, as a characteristic of thought, and therefore as a constituent principle of personality, or subjectivity. This self-knowing, as a principle, would underlie the preoccupations of those who wish to know themselves with their weakness and their greatness, in order to consolidate their virtue; and it would be perceived through a privileged, but transitory, insight within the *cogito*.

We can examine this tradition at a number of stages:

firstly, in Aristotle himself;

secondly, in the early neo-Platonists' use of Aristotle's theme within a platonist system, and Augustine's critique of it;

thirdly, with the later neo-Platonists' development of this theme, particularly with Proclus, and pseudo-Dionysius's critique of him;

fourthly, in the attitude taken to augustinian themes and to the limited proclean material available to St. Albertus Magnus and St. Thomas Aquinas, and the rediscovery of Proclus after Thomas and the association of themes of his

---

11. *Vide, Discours sur la Méthode*, 4, and *Méditations*, 2. From Descartes' letter CCXIX, to an unknown correspondent, of Nov., 1640, it appears that he did not take the idea from Augustine: v. *Oeuvres de Descartes*, edd. C. Adam and P. Tannery, 11 vols (Paris, 1897-1909), vol. 3, Correspondence (1899), pp. 247-8.

thought with those of St. Augustine and pseudo-Dionysius in a school of German Dominicans deriving from Albert, during the early fourteenth century; this was the first entrance of neo-Platonism into Germany;

fifthly, in the developments to the theme of self-knowing made in Fichte and Hegel, following on the critical philosophy of Kant, and in the rediscovery of neo-Platonism by Hegel and Schelling, which was its second entrance into Germany.

Finally, because of the dependence of Marx and Engels on Hegel, despite their opposition to his intellectualism, we shall see whether the same theme continues in them.

Aristotle thought that the difference of the nature of mind was apparent from its manifestations in the midst of the sensual life. For one could use the mind when one chose to, but the senses are only passive[12]; and while violent sensations deaden the senses, the mind's confrontation with what is most intelligible actually strengthens it.[13] On the objects of thought themselves, the νοητά, Aristotle's position was not always the same. In the *de Anima*, in the place of Plato's knowing through reminiscence, he made intellectual knowledge the creation of mind, which, once created, it would be

12. *De Anima* II, 5, 417b[24-6]: 'with intellectual knowledge it is within a man to use whenever he wishes; with sense knowledge it is not within him. The sense object must be there.'

13. *Ib*. III, 4, 429a[31]-b[5]: 'the sense power is not able to be sensitivized after violent sensation . . . but when mind thinks an intelligible with corresponding intensity, it is not less able to think of lessor objects, but more so. For the sensitive faculty is not outside the body, whereas the other is separate.'

6

able to receive into itself, and so, in principle, to become all things.[14] But in the *Metaphysics*, the νοητά are spoken of as pre-existent; for they move the mind.[15] Yet, with Aristotle there is no doubt that in actual knowing, mind and object are identified.[16]

The positions of the two works on self-knowing are compatible. In knowing other things, mind has the capacity of knowing itself,[17] for 'thought thinks itself through participation in the object of thought'.[18] And mind can give its attention to itself, for 'it is thinkable, just like other objects of thought'.[19] Conceived as separable from the human body, mind is described as 'immortal and eternal'[20], 'more divine',[21] and 'as something divine' in a man.[22] However, in making mind and its essential activity separable from the

14. *Ib*. III, 5, 430a[14-17] '(Mind) is then of such a nature as to become all things; on the other hand to make all things it has the character which is found in light. For it is in the manner of light to make colours existing potentially to be actual colours.'

15. *Metaphysics* XII, 7, 1072a[26-7,30]: 'the object of desire and the object of thought move without being moved . . . mind is moved by the intelligibles.'

16. *De Anima* III, 5, 430a[19-20]: 'actualised knowledge is the same as the object': *Metaphysics* XII, 7, 1072b[21]: 'mind and object of thought are the same.'

17. *De. Anima*., III, 4, 429b[5-7,9-10]: 'When, like a scholar actually excercising his knowledge, (the mind) has become each (object that it can know) . . . it then has the capacity to think itself.'

18. *Metaphysics* XII, 7, 1072b[20].'. . . because what is receptive of the object of thought, that is essence (τῆς οὐσίας), is mind,' (ib.[22]).

19. *De Anima* III, 4, 430a[2-3].

20. *Ib*. III, 5, 430a[22-23, 25]: 'Set free from this, alone, it is precisely what it is, and this "alone" is immortal and eternal . . . and outside of it nothing thinks.'

21. *Ib*. 1, 4, 408b[29].

22. *Nichomachaean Ethics* X, 7, 1177b[28].

body and divine, Aristotle prevented it from coordinating the activity of the sensual powers: a human subjectivity structure could not be based on it.[23] These texts, in which the mind is seen as divine: separable, though not yet separated from the restrictions of its embodiment, seem like anticipations of the self-thinking of the divine mind in *Metaphysics* XII, chapter 9. There, he arrived at his position not so much by intuition as by deduction. The divine thought cannot be determined by something else, and it must be about something unchangeable (for the opposite of both would entail potentiality); it will not be about something below it, or of something superior and better. It is, then, in a state of self-equality, with thinking as activity and as object: 'mind thinks itself, if it is what is best, and its thinking is a thinking of thinking.'[24]

Sublime, though problematic, this teaching represented but one area of Aristotle's concern. Because of its pure transcendence, divine self-knowing could not, by itself be imposed as a structural principle, bringing together all of his concerns, any more than it could, by itself, be made the co-ordinating centre of the human soul. Only through the use made by self-thinking in the synthesis of platonist and aristotelian thought in neo-Platonism, could self-thinking mind become a principle of structural unity in reality and in thought; and only with this transformation did it become a plausible central concern for western metaphysics.

---

23. *Vide*, Booth, 'St. Augustine's "notitia sui" ', II, pp. 109-11, 124-7, 129. Part II (pp. 104-32) considers the whole Aristotelian problematic of mind.

24. *Metaphysics* XII,9, 1074b[34-35] (and summarising from line 15).

For two hundred and fifty years most of Aristotle's corpus lay, undisturbed, in a cave at Skepsis. Once it began to circulate again[25] the disappointment must have been great. Only the dialogues of his Plato-period had been circulating, but the corpus now revealed another orientation, opposite, and sometimes overtly hostile, to Plato's. However, a closer examination of the text revealed a platonist vocabulary[26] which seemed to encourage a syncretism with Plato's thought, increasingly called for in order to conserve the philosophical tradition against the rising influence of the more unified Christian thought. Such a union was proposed in the oral teaching of Ammonius Saccas. Under pressure from his own circle, Plotinus, a pupil of Ammonius, put his own oral teaching into writing. This was later given its present thematic ordering as the *Enneads*, by his disciple, the apostate Christian, Porphyry.

The centre of Plotinus's system is the One; 'beyond thought and beyond being'[27], it is the cause and end of all. From the One proceeds the hypostasis of Mind. The One is in perfect self-equality. Mind desires this same self-equality, to know itself in the One from whom it derives,[28] and from

25. The whole story is told in P. Moraux, *Der Aristotelismus bei den Greichen*, vol. 1, *Peripatoi*, 5, (Berlin, 1973), pp. 3-44.

26. Aristotle used Plato's vacabulary to point the *difference* from his own theories: v. Booth, *Aristotlelian Aporetic Ontology in Islamic and Christian Thinkers*, Cambridge Studies in Medieval Life and Thought, 3rd series, 20, (Cambridge, 1983), p. 1.

27. *Ennead* V 1, 8. The 'One' derives from a theodician interpretation of Plato's *Parmenides*. It also has the characteristics of 'the Good' of the *Republic*, which 'exceeds being' (509B).

28. *Ennead* V 6, 5: 'To think is not primary as to both being and value, but takes second place. . . . In thinking the Good, it thinks itself by accident.'

whom it has fallen short.[29] The distance between the self it would know in the One and itself as knowing is the origin of an outflow of energy, which the desire to return to self-equality has revealed.[30] That energy produces a hypostasis of inferior power, designated as 'Soul', also intent on returning to itself in its source in Mind, and through that to the One, and also falling short[31]; and from this falling short is produced, from the lesser energy thus revealed, the material world.[32] Even the material world has a still remoter and weaker desire for the source of all, which is analogous to the infinitely intenser return, or conversion, of Mind and Soul. Mind is both intelligence and intelligible — but, at once, every intelligible, now identified with the ideas of Plato (whose 'life' is defined, in aristotelian fashion, as 'self-knowing'); it is 'One-many'[33]. Like Aristotle's divine thinking, it is aware of nothing else but itself. Soul, too, is self-knowing; yet while it looks with intensity, and forgetfulness of everything else, at its source in Mind, it must also preside over the material world; it is 'One-and-many'[34], for its particularisations — Soul in individuals — are more independent. Normally man exists in the sphere of Soul, but from

29. *Ib*. V 3,7: 'It knows itself, knowing that it comes from God. (v. V 3 *passim*.) On the reasons for the separation, cf *ib*, VI 7,15: 'it could not sustain the power poured upon it, and therefore broke it up and made it multiple in order to support it thus, part by part'; VI 9,5: 'It had the audacity to separate itself from the One'; VI 2,3: 'It is the fecundity of nature which makes the one a not-one'.

30. *Ib*. VI 7,17: 'In being generated, mind makes all other things appear.'

31. *Ib*. V 1,3; V 3,6; VI 9,3.

32. *Ib*. III 7,11. Soul produces the world on the model of Mind.

33. *Ib*. V 1,8.

34. *Ib*.

10

Soul he can turn to his source in Mind, which is 'our's when we use it'[35], and, through Mind, seek in ecstasy, identity with the One.[36]

Everything is seeking self-equality from different degrees of alienation, and the essential mind-life of a man is not the ascending dialectic and return to earth of Plato,[37] but an inverse movement as he discovers in himself a place in this conversion of all things, back to his source and back to himself.[38] Such is the prominence given to the aristotelian theme of self-thinking in its use by Plotinus; and such is its real beginning as a central theme in Western thinking.

How much of Plotinus was directly known to Augustine is difficult to say.[39] He reveals a direct knowledge of

35. *Ennead* V 3, 3.

36. In union with mind a man discovers that 'since he is in himself all things, in thinking himself he thinks at the same time all things': *ib*. IV 4, 2. For his union with the One ('to flee alone to the Alone'), v. *ib*. VI 9, 10-11.

37. Part enmythologised, the platonic élévation and return are beautifully described in *Phaedrus*, 246A-7E, where the references to soul and mind should be noted. Permanence with true reality is only for the Gods.

38. *Ennead* VI 9, 3: 'one must rise to the principle within oneself to become one instead of many. . . . One must become mind . . . to receive the object of the contemplation of mind.'

39. A. Solignac proposes parallels in the *Confessions*, v. *Oeuvres de Saint Augustin*, vols. 13 and 14 (Paris (and Bruges?), 1962). cf. Index in second vol., pp. 651-2; and v. especially notes in first vol., pp. 679-703. Augustine quotes him (freely) twice (IX 17, X 16), and cites him on a few other occasions, in *de Civitate Dei*. I have argued elsewhere that in *de Trinitate*, Augustine was systematically making a comprehensive restructuring of triadic and dyadic accounts of self-loving and self-knowing which are found in the *Enneads*: 'St. Augustine's "notitia sui" ', V, p. 104; but the nearness of similar conceptions in Porphyry is evident from the examples given (*ib*., pp. 97-121). His dying words ('He is not a great man who thinks it a great thing that beams and stones should fall, and mortal man should perish') allude to a passage in *Ennead* I 4, 7; but one could not be sure that he know it directly.

some texts of Porphyry[40]; he may have had a direct knowledge of other texts, as well as an indirect knowledge.[41] But any certainty about Augustine's knowledge of Porhyry is made difficult by the disappearance of so many of his works[42], by the fact that Augustine adapts neo-Platonist

40. He offers to Porphyry's Commentary on the Chaldaean Oracles (*de Civitate Dei*, XIX 23), his letter to Anebo (*ib.* X 11), and hs *de Regressu Animae* (*ib.* X 29). Perhaps Augustine was studying texts which he had never seen before, for a new apologetic problem, which passes over into *de Trinitate* from *de Civitate Dei* (cf. Booth, 'St. Augustine's "notitia sui" ', III pp. 366-369.

41. His reference to syncretists of Plato and Aristotle (*Contra Academicos*, III 19, 42), may refer to Porphyry's work *On the Unity of Plato and Aristotle*: v. J. Bidez, *Vie de Porphyre, le philosophe néoplatonicien*; (Ghent and Leipzig, 1913), p. 68*, no. (31-)32; R. Beutler, art. 'Porphyrios', Paulys-Wissowa, *Realencyclopädie der classischen Altertumswissenschaft*, XXII, 1 (1953), col. 285, no. 20. That he objected to a justification of idolatry in the books he acquired in Latin translation (*Confessions* VII 9, 15) might be a reference to Porphyry's *Contra Christianos* (fragments edited by A. Harnach, *Abhandlungen der königlichen Preussischen Akademie der Wissenschaften*, phil.-hist. Klasse, 1916, 1; v. fr. 76, pp. 92f; and cf. Italían transl. by C. Mutti, *Porfirio, Discorsi contra i cristiani*, (Padua, 1977), at same no.: pp. 139-41). Harnack also asserts (pp. 17, 94 - i.e. fr. 79) that Augustine refers to the work in Letter 102, 16. This entails interpreting 'inquit' as being said by Porphyry, and the passage cited there certainly refers to the argument at the end of fr. 76: that idolatry is practiced by Christians, or is sanctioned by primitive practice. But in this letter, Augustine may be replying to objections of Porphyry, repeated elsewhere: cf. (Letter) 102, 8: 'alia proposuerunt, quae dicerent de Porphyrio contra Christianos tanquam validiora *decerpta*'; and *ib.*, 30: 'nec ipsa *quasi* ex Porphyrio, sed tanquam ex irrisione paganorum'. Augustine compared the triads of Porphyry with those of Plotinus, but gave no references: *de Civitate Dei*, X 23. cf. also Booth, 'St. Augustine's "notitia sui" ', III, pp. 392-5, espec. n. 146, and cf. ib., I, p. 76, n. 18.

42. They were ordered to be burnt in 448: *Codex Iustiniani*, I 1, 3.

12

ideas as he uses them[43], and because Porphyry's ideas are normally near to those of Plotinus.[44] According to Augustine's *Confessions*, during his heart- and mind-searching period before his conversion '(God) procured for me, by means of a man inflated with extraordinary pride, certain books of the Platonists translated into Latin'[45]. And, 'ad-

43. E.g., *de Civitate Dei* X 23: '(Porphyry) refers to God the Father and God the Son . . . ' . The process may have begun in doxography and translations. Macrobius's *Commentary on the 'Dream of Scipio'* (summarizing Plotinus) does not represent the hypostatic nature of Soul by describing it as 'fount of all souls' (I 6,20); and Roman readers, used to the use of 'mens' for the transcendent divine, would not be alerted to all the qualities of Plotinus's 'Mind' (I 14,6ff).

44. We can here only note the difference between Beutler, that he did not fundamentally alter the principles of Plotinus (art. cit. coll. 301-2), and W. Theiler, that he made the cosmos anthropocentric, with a metaphysics of basically human and ethical orientation ('Porphyrius und Augustin', in *Forschungen zum Neo-Platonismus*, Quelle und Studien zur Geschichte der Philosophie, 10 (Berlin, 1966), p. 171, (originally in *Schriften der Königsberger Gelehrten Gesselschaft*, Geist.wiss. klasse 10, 1933). With the latter, A.C. Lloyd, in a qualified way, approves: *Later Greek and Early Medieval Philosophy*, ed. A.H. Armstrong, (Cambridge, 1967, reprinted 1980), p. 288.

45. *Confessions* VII 9,13. He names no authors; and where one might expect 'Plotinus' later (VII 19,25), the *Corpus Christianorum* apparatus has no doubts about 'Photini'. If Porphyry's *Contra Christianos* were among the books (v. supra, n. 41), it could be that a pagan intellectual was intent on stopping Augustine's conversion. This account is not entirely compatible with that in *de Beata Vita*, 1,4, where he speaks of reading 'some few' works of *Plotinus* (v. *Corpus Christianorum* text at p. 67[99]: the reading is not unanimous), lent by Manlius Theodorus, to whom this work is dedicated. It cannot be shown that this lender was the man 'inflated with extraordinary pride'. Then were there two lenders? Arguing from Augustine's *Retractiones* (I,2), where he says he had overpraised this man ('quamvis docto et Christiano viro, plus tribui quam deberem'), Courcelle thinks that the same person is referred to: *Recherches sur les Confessions de s. Augustin*, 2nd edn., (Paris, 1968), pp. 153-6, 281-4). The translator was Marius Victorinus: cf. *Confessions* VIII 2,3.

monished by these books to return to myself, I entered into the intimacy of myself under your guidance, and I was able to do so because you have become my helper. I entered, and I saw, with whatever eye of my soul, above the same eye of my soul, the unchangeable light'[46]. A conversion to oneself, and through that conversion, a conversion to God, characterises the teaching of Plotinus and Porphyry,[47] but that does not in itself raise the problem of a neo-Platonist conversion separable from his Christian conversion.[48] For Augustine, conversion was wholly a grace,[49] even though it

46. *Confessions* VII 10, 16; cf. VII 20,26: 'admonished by them to seek the incorporeal truth'.

47. Formularies as trenchant as Augustine's 'God, always the same, I would know myself, I would know thee' (*Soliloquies* II 1,1) are found in both Plotinus (*Enneads* V 1,1, 8.11; VI 5,12, 7,37,9,2), and Porphyry (*Sententiae* : (XIII), (XXX), XL, XLII, XLIII (following numeration of B. Mommert (Leipzig, 1907: Bibliotheca Teubneriana)).

48. The long debate is summarized in A. Schindler, art. 'Augustin/Augustinismus I', *Theologische Realenzyklopädie*, vol. 4 (Berlin, 1979), pp. 660-2. J.-M. le Blond is undoubtedly correct in saying that Augustine's platonism was 'revised, purified, vivified by his faith in Christ' (*Les Conversions de Saint Augustin*, (Paris, 1950), p. 138; but the distinction of two conversions exaggerates a merely pedagogical distinction. cf. *Confessions* VII 21,27: 'I began to read (the Scriptures and especially St. Paul), and I discovered that whatever truth I had read (in the platonists) was said here with the commendation of your grace.' That seems to entail that the progress of his conversion had been helped by reading these works differently from their author's intentions.

49. The position is repeated in innumerable texts, of which one may cite *Sermon 2 on Psalm LXX*, 2: 'From which I am converted to you, made new by you — I who was made by you, recreated — I who was created, reformed — I who was formed; no merit of mine can be said to have preceded my being converted, but your grace has gratuitously come to me, so that I might be mindful of your justice alone.' Even the possibility of grace was from God: v. *de Gratia Christi* I 3,4 (PL 44.362).

might be given gradually.[50] His encounter with the neo-Platonist works occurred between his enrollment as a cate-chumen,[51] at the beginning of a conversion which he said himself was slow,[52] and the final crisis of tears with the 'tolle, lege . . . ' in the garden.[53] In this sixteenth centenary of his conversion, whose consequences have so affected our history, we can discern within it the dimensions of neo-Platonist conversion, that while it is a return to the highest reality above the human mind, it is also a confrontation with the deepest reality within it.

About twenty-five years later, Augustine had an en-counter with neo-Platonism which was more disputatious. The *de Civitate Dei*, which he was slowly writing, begins in the middle to take on an anti-neo-Platonist polemic, per-haps as a consequence of Augustine's meeting with 'cul-tured pagan noblemen of Rome (who) had begun to make their presence felt, as refugees, in the *salons* of Carthage,[54] after the Vandal capture of Rome in 410. A change is also

50. *On Various Questions, to Simplicianus*, I 2,2: 'it may be the case with some that a fuller and more evident grace may be infused with the passage of time or the celebration of the sacraments . . . with some, as with catechumens, the grace of faith is such that it is not enough to gain the kingdom of heaven, as with Cornelius, before he was incorporated into the Church by participating in the sacraments; with others it is so great that already they may be accounted as in the body of Christ, in the holy Temple of God.'

51. *Confessions* V 14,25.

52. *Ib.* VI 11,20: 'I delayed to be converted to the Lord.'

53. *Ib.* VIII 8,19 - end.

54. P. Brown, *Augustine of Hippo*, (London, 1967), p. 300. Por-phyry is first mentioned in VII 25, and the discussion of Platonism begins in VIII.

apparent in the middle of the *de Trinitate*,[55] which was being written at the same time, as he constructed an apologetic for the Christian Trinity, related on the one hand to Sacred Scripture and on the other to a set of new philosophical concepts.

That this second part of the *de Trinitate* should not be regarded as under the 'influence' of neo-Platonist writings,[56] but as another anti-neo-Platonist apologetic has been argued elsewhere.[57] His arguments use models drawn from the inter-relation of the faculties, and their acts, in human knowing to suggest the truth of the Christian doctrine. But the models themselves are important for providing an account of the structure of human subjectivity, which was dominant until the challenge of renaissance scientism,[58] and

55. *Vide*, Booth, 'St. Augustine's "notitia sui" ', III, pp. 366-9. VIII marks a new beginning; IX begins the exposition. Its opening words imply that he could have written about other triads: 'Our intention is to make an investigation of the Trinity, not about any and every (non quamlibet: sc. Trinity/triad), but about the Trinity which God is, the true, highest and only God' (IX 1,1).

56. As it has been, notably by O. du Roy: v. Booth, 'St. Augustine's "notitia sui" ', I, p. 103, n. 105; for other authors, cf. *ib*. III, 390-6. 'Influence' should be used as a model for intellectual relationships only when much more than a mere contact is detectable; the creative response of the recipient may far outweigh the original reception.

57. *Vide*, *ib*. pp. 102-4; but this emerges from the whole study.

58. *Vide*, H. Heimsoeth, *Die sechs grossen Themen der abendlandischen und der Ausgang des Millelalters*, (Berlin, 1922), p. 137: 'In fact with his teaching on the self-certainty of consciousness, he laid the foundations for a thousand years' development.'

whose power is clear from subsequent revivals. Some of the models involve self-knowing, and bring Augustine for a second time into the tradition we are examining.

Whilst giving an account of the Christian Trinity which is clearer than that of the neo-Platonist account of their triad of hypostases, his account conserved the separateness of the human individual from the transcendent Godhead, especially when he gave to the memory a function of correlating all the human powers together, which neither the empiricism of Aristotle nor the transcendentalism of neo-Platonism had been able to do. Although one finds elements from neo-Platonist thought, they have been thoroughly restructured: though his message is different, the apologist has to speak the language of his opponents. Whilst the Greek intellectual milieu had become instinctively philosophical, Romanitas remained legalistic: it looked on the individual as a bearer of rights, and its own native Stoicism looked at the individual's concern for virtue. The Roman conception of *mens*, which even for the divine connoted an individual mind, would remove any transcendence or ambiguity in νοῦς and ψυχή. Augustine's Romanitas, and his rhetor experience, predisposed him not to accept, or not to see, the trans-subjective structure accorded to the human personality by neo-Platonism.

According to neo-Platonist theory, mind was striving to realise its nature and be in equality with itself, and its falling short of this was the origin of its productivity and the consequent multiplicity. According to Augustine, whenever mind was knowing itself, it was always knowing the totality of itself, the wholeness of itself, even though it could not know the totality of things in itself. He plays the 'tota mens' which it knows against the 'totum in mente' which it does not.[59] But how could the mind really know any part of this *totum*, unless it first knew, as a principle of this *totum*, itself as *tota*? Against the ascent of the human individual into the transcendence of mind in neo-Platonism, Augustine's conception of the equality of the mind as knowing to the mind known as *tota* furnishes a self-certainty and a positive valuation for the human mind, and thereby for the whole human being, in whatever condition, and with a consequent openness to a total and veritable reception of transcendence.

He says that at first self-knowing comes from deliberation, with the mind placing itself before itself.[60] In this way self-knowing takes on the triadic form which is found with other acts of knowledge,[61] with will or love uniting the subject to the object known.[62] But, on close examination, it becomes clear that the mind does not have to confront itself

59. *De Trinitate*, X 4,6: 'it is absurd to claim that the mind does not know as a whole what it knows. I do not say that it knows all, but that what it knows it knows as a whole. When, therefore, it knows something of itself, which it cannot know except as a whole, it knows itself as a whole. But it knows itself as knowing something, and it cannot know something except as a whole. Therefore it knows itself as a whole.' cf. *ib.* IX 4,7: 'when mind knows the whole of itself (se totam), that it knows (itself) perfectly, its knowledge is throughout all of itself (per tortum eius)'. This self-equality in all self-knowing contrasts with the need for a preliminary complete knowledge of (the ?) soul in Plotinus: 'We do not know all that passes in any part of the soul before having arrived at the complete (knowledge) of the soul (εἰς ὅλην τὴν ψυχὴν)' (*Ennead* IV 8,8).

60. *De Trinitate* XIV 6,8: 'so great is the power of thinking (cogitationis vis) that not even the mind itself may place itself, so to speak, in its own sight, except when it thinks itself (quando se cogitat)'.

61. cf Booth, 'St. Augustine's "notitia sui" ', V, pp. 112-3, n. 54.

62. *De Trinitate, ib*; 'that by which both are joined, love or will. . . . they are joined by a third (factor) of delight, which is none other than the will enjoying something, desiring it or possessing it.'

afresh, but is always known to itself.[63] This continuity comes from its nature. Taking the full scope of the Roman conception of *mens*, he says that love and knowledge are substantially identical with mind.[64] And so, 'the mind itself, its love and its knowledge are three things, and these three are one; and when they are perfect they are equal.'[65] Hence, whatever is considered by mind is reached by its knowing and loving. But the mind is primarily self-knowing and self-loving, for if self-loving were to cease there would be no loving of anything else, and if self-knowing were to cease, there would be no knowing of anything else;[66] and this does not suffer from being placed in a world of time, because the

63. *Ib.*: 'I cannot discover how, when it does not think itself, it may not be in sight of itself, since it can never be without itself, as if it were one thing itself and its sight (of itself) were another. . . . Or is it so to speak doubled . . . so that in itself it is seeing, and in front of itself is seen? ' Thus there are two different situations for self-knowing: a self-knowing which is continual, which is at the base of subjectivity, and the acts in which the mind deliberately turns its attention to itself. cf. *ib*. XIV 7,9: 'aliud esse rem quamque non nosse, aliud non cogitare.'

64. *Ib.* IX 4,5: 'love and knowledge are not in the mind as in a subject, but they are there substantially, like mind itself.' cf. *Ib*. IX 2,2: 'Nor are love and mind two spirits, but one spirit; not two essences, but one.' For this and what follows, cf. Booth, 'Augustine's "notitia sui" ', IV, pp. 206-11.

65. *Ib*. IX 4,4.

66. *Ib*. IX 5,6: 'if the love by which the mind loves itself ceases to be, then (the mind) itself will at the same time also cease to love. Likewise, if the knowledge by which the mind knows itself ceases to be, then (the mind) itself will at the same time cease to know.' Note that the reading accepted by the critical *Corpus Christianorum* edition (p. 298[56-7]), and by Migne, is: 'simul et illa nosse *se* desinit'. I have suppressed that 'se', which is added interlinearly in one and omitted from another of the best MSS. Its presence entails a pointless duplication (se mens novit = nosse se). The knowing is co-existensive with the range of the mind (v. text at n. 65). With the 'se', the symmetry of the thought is lost.

memory, which is the correlate of duration and the co-ordinator of all experience, allows the mind to scrutinise itself in time and over time.[67] Provided that every sense- and bodily-related experience, with their burden of imagery, is discarded, the true self will be known[68] in a nucleus of self-knowing, self-loving and self-remembering: each power comprehending itself and comprehending the others; yet their essence is the same self, distendible in time through the memory.[69]

At the same time a valid image of the divine Trinity of Christian faith, and unmistakably human, wherever these reflections of Augustine were diffused, whether in whole or

67. In contrast to neo-Platonism, which was consistent in despising the human memory: v. *Ennead* IV 3,32; 4.4. cf. Booth, 'St. Augustine's "notitia sui" ', IV, p. 215.

68. *De Trinitate* X 8,11: 'it will see that there never was a time when it did not love itself, and never a time when it did not know itself; but because it loved another thing with itself, it has confused itself with this other thing. *ib.* 10,16:' if it adds nothing from these thoughts (of material things) to itself, so as to regard itself as something of the kind, then whatever still remains to it of itself, that alone is itself.' The latter passage is reminiscent of Husserl's more complex ἐπωχή; the I is revealed in a transcendental-phenomenological ἐπωχή after ἐπωχή has reduced the world to a stream of 'cogitationes': v. §§ 11 and 15 of *Cartesianische Meditationen*, in *Husserliana* 1, (The Hague, 1950); transl. by Dorian Cairns, *Cartesian Meditations*, (The Hague, 1977) (6th impression).

69. *De Trinitate* X 11,18: 'For I remember that I have a memory, understanding and will; and I understand that I understand, will and remember; and I will that I will, remember and understand; and at the same time I remember my whole memory, understanding and will. . . . Wherefore when all are mutually comprehended by each one, and are comprehended as wholes, there each one as a whole is equal to each other one as a whole, and each one as a whole is equal to all together as wholes; and all these are one life, one mind and one essence.' cf. Booth, 'St. Augustine's "notitia sui" ', V. pp. 109-10.

in part or in doxography, they established or confirmed a view of human personality that we can still accept today. Were all the resources within its conceptual simplicity better known and pondered, its utility would still be recognised; for in this feverish world, no man can be indifferent to its provocation to know himself as a self.

Whilst the works of Augustine were being copied and summarized in Roman centres, the tradition of pagan neo-Platonist philosophy continued in the 'university' centres of Athens, Alexandria and Constantinople in the East. It blossomed strikingly in Proclus, a critical follower of Plotinus, Porphyry and others. His most remarkable work was the *Platonic Theology*: a speculative discernment of an identical supra-sensible structure, under different names, in all of Plato's dialogues.[70]

The source of all is again the One — beyond being, known, under its desirable aspect, as 'the Good'.[71] Below the One are the transcendent Gods: intelligible, intelligible-intellective and intellective, which, excepting the last member, which is single, would make up a triad of triads of

70. So far only the first four books have appeared in the Budé edition (Greek critical text with French translation): *Proclus, Théologie Platonicienne*, edited and translated by H.D. Saffrey and L.G. Westerink, (Paris, 1968 —), designated here as 'S-W'. So the complete text remains the first edition: *Procli Successoris Platonici, in Platonis Theologiam Libri Sex*, edited by Aemilius Portus, (Hamburg, 1618; photographically reprinted, Frankfurt am Main, 1960), with Latin translation and other contents. S-W gives the Portus pagination in its page-heads and text. The English translation by T. Taylor: *The Six Books of Proclus . . . On the Theology of Plato*, etc., 2 vols. (London, 1816) is difficult to come by.

71. *Id.*, II 6, S-W p. 40^{25-7}: 'the Good is the converter of all the derivative (beings), whilst the One is the giver of existence.'

21

triads. From a rarified interpretation of the dialogues, Proclus declared certain metaphysical principles to be divine: 'finite', 'infinite', their 'mixture', and then 'being', 'life', 'mind', make up the two higher triads of triads; and at the lower level of the second are the divinised forms.[72] Only among the intellective Gods of the third triad do we encounter names from classical mythology. After these transcendent triads are the Gods of the world, arranged in three orders as hypercosmic, hypercosmic-encosmic and encosmic. The highest triad of triads — of 'finite' (or limit), 'infinite' (or illimit), and their 'mixture' — has the same three elements, with one predominating in each triad. At the summit is the 'mixed'. In the triad in which it predominates, it is the being of being, and participated by everything; in the second triad it is the being of life; and in the third the being of intellect.[73] The first of these triads is characterised by stability; the second triad by stability and procession; the third triad is the counterpart to procession: it converts what has proceeded back to its source, for 'the conversion to and the coincidence with the intelligible belongs universally to mind.'[74] On this triad of triads of Gods depends the structure, which is the activity, of the resultant other hierarchies

72. *Id.*, IV 14, S-W pp. 43-5. For outline plan of whole pantheon, v. S-W, I, pp. LX-LXXV.

73. The triad derives from Plato's *Philebus*, 23 C-D. For the first 'mixed': 'being itself ($\alpha\dot{v}\tau o o \nu$) and nothing other than being', III 9, S-W p. 35^{6-7}; 'primary being', *id.*, S-W p. 38^{23}; 'all things in a hidden way', *id.*, S-W p. 39^{3-4}; 'the being of being', *id.*, III 11, S-W p. 43^{25-6}. For the second 'mixed': the being of intelligible life, III 12, S-W p. 46^{13-20}. For the third 'mixed': the being of intelligible intellect, *id.*, III 14, S-W p. 51^{7-19}.

74. *Id.*, III 14, p. 50^{4-13}.

22

of Gods, and ultimately of the material universe.[75]

Though there are expressions of the mind's nature being to return upon itself,[76] the converting function of the lower intellects, under the causality of the higher triads, is assimilated into the conversion of all things by desire to the One.[77] In fact, Proclus is more concerned with being, than to reduce being to an activity of transcendent mind. Quoting Plato's *Phaedo*, he professes himself as 'on the hunt for being'[78], and 'being in its truest being' ($\tau\grave{o}$ '$\acute{o}\nu\tau os$'$\acute{o}\nu$): the 'really real' he identifies with the intelligible — which is the nature of the transcendent intelligible Gods.[79] Therefore the intelligible is to be identified with being, for the intelligible itself is intelligible through its being, and 'every intellect is also a dispenser of knowledge and every intelligible is a dispenser of being'.[80] By the reduction of intelligible and intel-

75. E.g., the intelligible Gods (triads of finite, infinite and mixture) 'assure the perfection of the limits, peaks and existences of all things': *id.* IV 38, S-W, p. 110[24-6].

76. They are most rare (cf. II 4, S-W p. 36[22-3]; IV 38, S-W p. 110[12-5]). But it contributes to an overall notion of 'conversion'.

77. *Id.*, III 4, S-W p. 16[5-14]: 'all things tend towards the primary cause of the whole . . . . (Likeness) introduces kinship among the many, together with sympathy and a friendship for each other and the One.' cf. supra, at n. 71.

78. Quoting the *Phaedo* (66C) at the beginning of his preface: S-W (I), p. 5[14-5]; repeated at I 9, S-W p. 40[9-10]; I 26, S-W p. 113[14]; IV 6, S-W p. 22[24]. The 'hunt' begins with a return to oneself, for mind and the hierarchy of being are in the soul: I 3, S-W pp. 15[21]-16[18].

79. Cf., *ib.*, IV 1, S-W p. 8[7-9]. I 26, S-W p. 118[4-9] warns that 'intelligible' is used for all the orders, but of the divine it is not used in this sense.

80. *Ib.*, IV 13, S-W p. 43[8-13].

23

lect to being,[81] the cosmos is an emanation of being and of knowledge reduced to being through descending hierarchical levels, and their return, as being, to their source;[82] not through a movement in which everything is simplified according to the nature of mind, but in a hierarchy of distinguished dependences.[83] On this point Proclus specifically separates himself from Plotinus.[84] As we shall see,[85] Hegel was extremely interested in Proclus's triad of triads of intelligible Gods, because reality was to him the union of universal (or unlimited) and individual (or limited); but here he reinterpreted Proclus's identity of being and intelligible as an identity of, and in, pure thought.

Proclus summed up the teaching of the *Platonic Theology* in his *Theological Elements*, which later in the Arab world and in Western Christendom reached a wider public.

81. *Ib.*, IV 36, S-W p. 106^{24-26}: 'the One is beyond the nature of mind, whilst being gives existence to mind, and the mind is nothing other than being.' For the intelligible as being, cf. III 9, SW p. 35^{8-9}: 'we have shown that primary being embraces all things intelligibly, including life and intellect'.

82. For this exitus-reditus, v. *ib.* II 7, S-W p. 45^{14-24}, and espec. III 9, S-W p. 35^{8-24}.

83. The hierarchical nature of the emanation is clear from III 6, S-W p. 28^{3-21}.

84. *Vide, ib.* I 10, espec. S-W pp. 42^4-43^{21}; he says he is following Syrianus in this. His says that his dialectic corresponds with, and imitates, the procession and conversion of being: I 9, S-W p. 40^{1-18}: cf. IV 27, S-W p. 78^{10-13}. cf. also III 27, SW p. 97^{16}-98^9: 'each form is at the head of a series'. Plotinus is probably meant again at IV 9, S-W p. 28^{7-10}.

85. *Vide*, infra, p. 000.

Theses of the self-conversion of intellectual substances[86] are found with other theses on their combination with other substances in terms of proceeding from and converting towards the same source[87], being filled with it and participating it[88], so that source is known with self[89]. It is more important as a text on being and emanation than on self-knowing, despite its unmatchably terse proposition: 'All that is capable of self-knowledge is capable of every form of self-conversion' (prop. 83). Without the *Platonic Theology*, the theogenic content of the *Elements* was not clear, and it was applied at a more material level of reality. Hence, its presence can be seen in a modest theory of intelligible substrates to the material world.[90]

Therefore, Proclus's thought was of hierarchical emanations of being, of which the corresponding hierarchised

86. (The translation of E.R. Dodds, *Proclus, The Elements of Theology,* (2nd edn, Oxford, 1963) (text, transl., introdn. and commentary) is not always followed.) v. prop. 15: 'Every thing that has the power to convert itself to itself is incorporeal'; prop. 83: v. infra in text; prop. 171 com.: 'that intelligence is incorporeal is shown by its conversion to itself'.

87. *Vide*, prop. 31: 'all that procedes from any principle, in respect of its being, converts to that from which it procedes.'

88. *Vide*, prop. 28 com.: 'the participated bestows upon the participant communion in that which it participates'; prop. 64 com.: '(complete substances) make the participants belong to them: for being complete, they fill the participants with themselves (prop. 25), and establish them in themselves.'

89. *Vide*, prop. 167: 'each intelligence subsequent (to the One) knows simultaneously itself and what is prior to it, so that its object is in part itself but in part its source.'

90. As in al-Kindī: v. Booth, *Aristotelian Aporetic Ontology*, pp. 91-2; Isaac Israeli, *ib*. pp. 92-3; Ibn Gabirol, *ib*. p. 169, n.21. There is also a significant editorial comment to this effect in a widely distributed collection of extracts from the 'Elements', translated into arabic (v. *ib*. pp. 88-9).

return, or conversion, through self-knowing minds was a function.

Proclus had successors at Athens and Alexandria, but their teaching was suppressed by Justinian. It produced a Christian riposte in the work on *The Divine Names*, by the pseudonymous Dionysius,[91] whose reduction of the three emanations of being, life and intelligence to a single emanation of being lies behind St. Thomas's conception; and it facilitated the inclusion of everything in a conversion to God.[92] The *Elements* were known in the West through the Latin translation finished in 1268.[93] Only then was it realised that the *Liber de Causis*, a monotheised, edited arabic version of some of its theses — including that of the intellect's conversion to itself[94] — and translated into Latin in the twelfth century[95], was derived from them.

91. It is a critical re-working of Proclus's 'Platonic Theology' I, part 2 (S-W, pp. 59-125).

92. This conception of being is united, in Thomas, with conceptions from Boethius and Ibn Rushd: v. booth, op. cit. (n. 90), pp. 78, 200, 201-2, 257. Of the five locations of ἐπιστροφή in the *Divine Names*, listed by P. Chevallier, O.S.B., in *Dionysiaca* (2 vols. (Paris-Bruges, 1937-49)), vol. 2, p. 1590, the first four are of conversions between levels of being, though within the context of God's power (showing a link with Proclus?), whilst the fifth is of the conversion of all things to God (Chevallier, p. 478 = Migne PG 3, 916D): thus the notion was available from pseudo-Dionysius.

93. By William de Moerbeke. 'The first to receive an exemplar of the new translation was Thomas Aquinas': H. Boese, 'Wilhelm von Moerbeke als Übersetzer der Stoicheiosis theologike des Proclus', *Abhandlungen der Heidelberger Akademie der Wissenschafen*, Philosoph.-historische Klasse, 1985, Abhandlung 5, p. 48.

94. Props. 7 and 15 speak of the intellect's 'return' to its essence ('reditio', 'redit', 'rediens').

95. Translated at Toledo by Gerard of Cremona, who died in 1187.

The Latin Christian culture up to the thirteenth century was scriptural, and patristic in that it was dominated by the great volume of works of Augustine. A very few texts of Plato, and rather more of Christian, or at least monotheised, neo-Platonism, together with a logic drawn from Aristotle and Boethius, gave the impression of coherence. To those able to compare it with other traditions, it seemed distinctly platonist.[96]

St. Albertus Magnus was the first to undertake the coordination of this tradition with the newly arrived arabic and Greek culture, which included neo-Platonist as well as aristotelian texts. So, to the small traces of Proclus, came crypto-Proclean works; and to the *Liber de Causis* from the arabic should be added the corpus of pseudo-Dionysius, only really accessible through a new Latin translation, completed in 1167.[97]

Albert's not surprising platonising syncretism, without a knowledge of Proclus's text,[98] brought logic together with emanation;[99] but this flux of reality from God, thought of under the image of light, found its *term* in the creation of

96. *Vide*, the praise given by Augustine to Plato in *de Civitate Dei* (VIII 12), where Aristotle is described as his 'disciple'.

97. *Cf.*, E. Booth, 'A Confrontation between the neo-Platonisms of St. Thomas Aquinas and Hegel', *Angelicum*, 63 (1968), pp. 68-9.

98. *Cf.*, *Platonic Theology* IV 27, S-W p. 78[10-11]: 'the links and connections of reasonings imitate that indissoluble one of things.'

99. Quite independently, A. de Libera and I came to a similar conclusion about his bringing together Ibn Sīnā's logic with emanation. cf. de Libera's 'privileged encounter between the logic of Avicenna and that of Albert the Great' ('Théorie des universaux et réalisme logique chez Albert le Grand', *Revue des Sciences Philosophiques et Théologiques*, 65 (1981), p. 69), and my '(Albert's) Neoplatonising interpretation put on Ibn Sīnā's ontology' (*Aristotelian Aporetic Ontology*, p. 167).

material things.[100] He knew of pseudo-Dionysius's conception of a conversion of all things to God,[101] but it is an idea hardly developed: it is seen as a reduction of things, as in logic, back to their first principles,[102] or, in a generalised way, as the movement of things to their ends. In no way does he take up the proclean theme of the intellect's returning to itself, commenting that a self-knowing which knows that from which it comes, or that which derives from it, is a more perfect self-knowing.[103] In an emanation scheme of great beauty, Albert elevated being to intellectuality;[104] but he gave no importance to the theme of self-knowing outside the places in the commentaries.[105]

100. Albert on *Liber de Causis, Opera Omnia* X, (Paris, 1891), p. 416b: 'It flows into that which has a terminus: . . . the termini are what define it . . . (and so on until it reaches something) outside whose termini it cannot overflow.'

101. 'Convertens ad seipsum omnia' (cf. supra, n. 92). v. *Super Dionysius de Divinis Nominibus, Opera Omnia* XXXVII.1, (Münster, 1972), p. 397b, where he equates it with 'reditus' (the term used by the *Liber de Causis*), which occurs a number of times in the work.

102. *Vide*, on *Liber de Causis*, p. 461b: 'a resolution back from effect to cause'. v. also on *de Coelesti Hierarchia Opera Omnia* XIV, (Paris, 1892), pp. 8a, 10a-b, 105a.

103. On *Liber de Causis*, p. 525b: 'In understanding itself absolutely (as they say) it does not understand its being and essence according to the perfect principle of being and essence.'

104. Form is a 'simple splendour', cognate to the 'splendour of the intellect': the texts are very striking, but difficult to present briefly: v. Booth, *Aristotelian Aporetic Ontology*, pp. 166-70, 181, 184-5, 187, 200, 201 n. 135. On the origin of matter, Albert is not precise: cf. *ib.* p. 176 and n. 44.

105. Besides on *Liber de Causis* II, chs. 31-34 (pp. 525-30), v. *Metaphysica, Opera Omina* XVI.II, (Münster, 1964), 11.2, ch. 30 (pp. 520a-522b).

Albert's pupil, St. Thomas, always saw intellectuality in function of being: being, not in the sense of the intelligible being of Proclus, but the single communication of all reality to a creature, of pseudo-Dionysius. The Latin 'esse' translates the Greek infinitive; but the English 'being' substantivises the verbal form too much.[106] Citing a passage in Augustine's *de Trinitate*, Thomas says that '(God's) to be is his to know';[107] and of created things he says that their union together in mind compensates for the imperfection of the separation of one being from another.[108]

At the beginning of the *Summa Theologiae*, Thomas announced a scheme of 'exitus-reditus' to cover the whole

106. Cf. Booth, *Aristotelian Aporetic Ontology*, p. 222 n. 74.

107. *Summa Theologiae* I 14,5 corp.: 'suum esse (est) suum intelligere.' He cites *de Trinitate* in the sed contra of 14,4: 'Deo hoc est esse, quod sapientem esse.' Augustine's text has 'hoc est ibi esse quod sapere' (VII 1,2), and 'hoc est Deo esse quod sapere' (VII 4,9).

108. *Quaestiones Disputatae de Veritate* 2,2 corp.: 'Note, therefore, that a thing is perfect in two ways. First, it is perfect with respect to the perfection of its being (esse), which belongs to it according to its own species. But since the specific being of one thing is distinct from the specific being of another, in every created thing of this kind, the perfection falls short of absolute perfection to the extent to which that perfection is found in other species. Consequently, the perfection of each individual thing considered in itself is imperfect, being a part of the perfection of the entire universe, which arises from the sum total of the perfections gathered together of individual things. In order that there might be some remedy for this imperfection, another kind of perfection is to be found in created things. It consists in this, that the perfection belonging to one thing is found in another. This is the perfection of a knower insofar as he is knowing; for something is known by a knower by reason of the fact that the thing known is, in some fashion, with the knower. Hence, it is said in III *De Anima* that the soul is, "in some manner, all things", since it was born to know all things. In this way it is possible that the perfection of the entire universe may exist in one thing.'

29

work,[109] but this is not linked in neo-Platonist fashion with God's knowing, since God 'knows everything in His own knowing' (which is His self-knowing and His essence), 'seeing them in Himself'.[110] The *Liber de Causis* expression of an intellectual creature's self-knowing as a 'return upon itself', he said was a metaphor,[111] and he gives it an ontological significance: 'to return to its essence is nothing other than for a thing to subsist in itself.'[112]

Perhaps because he thought that an ontological foundation was profounder and truer than one of knowing, he did not take up Augustine's model of self-knowing for the Trinity; though he sums up the whole *de Trinitate*, seemingly not accepting the role Augustine gave to the me-

109. *Vide*, Prologue to I, q.2. Note that there are two modes of conversion here: through a man's moral activity, which includes the exercise of the gifts of the Holy Spirit, (Part II), and through Christ and the sacraments (Part III). A.Patfoort, O.P., has shown that this is a generalisation, and that the text in detail does not conform to it: *Thomas d'Aquin: les clés d'une théologie*, (Paris, 1983), ch. 3. Thomas had proposed a similar relationship for the works of Boethius: v. Prologue to *Expositio super Librum Boethii*.

110. *Summa Theologiae* I 14,4 and 5. cf. *ib*. 6, corp.: 'God would not know himself perfectly unless he were to know whatever way his perfections are participable by others; nor also would he know perfectly the true nature of being, unless he were to know all modes of being.'

111. *Quaestiones Disputatae de Veritate*, 2,2 ad 2. Outside his own late commentary he rarely cites its propositions: v. R. Busa, S.J., *Index Thomisticus*, (Stuttgart-Bad Cannstatt, 1974-80), Sectio II, Concord. Prima, vol. 19, coll. 189a-191a: 'redire', etc.; Concord. Altera, vol. 5, col. 113a: 'reditio'.

112. *Summa Theologiae* I 14,2 ad 1. Thomas passes through the analyses of Aristotle, Averroes and Avicenna (i.e. Ibn Rushd and Ibn Sīna), to show not so much a God devoid of potentiality in knowing, as knowing and known to Himself without restriction: v. *de Veritate* 2,2 corp.; cf. *Summa Theologiae*, I 14,2 corp.

mory.[113] Instead he developed Augustine's other image of
the production of an 'inner word' in a man, and the com-
plaisance which follows, as an image of the Son and Holy
Spirit.[114]

Albert's overtly neo-Platonist thought was passed on to
an important 'school' of German Dominican philosophical
theologians, quite distinct from the Paris tradition, whose
writings are only now being studied and assessed.[115] They
stand as intermediaries between Albert and the better
known 'Rhineland mystics'; though Eckhart was both mys-
tic and theologian.[116] Undoubtedly Albert is the inspirer of

113. *In I Sententiarum*, Dist. 3, q.4, art.4, corp. Augustine is not
mentioned by name in the corpus. Thomas points out that, in learning for
the first time, knowing precedes remembering — which indicates disquiet
at the central role which Augustine gave to memory.

114. *Vide*, *Quaestiones Disputatae de Potentia*, 9,9, espec. corp.:
' . . . cum amor non sit aliud quam *stabilimentum* voluntatis in bono
volito.'

115. *Vide*, A. de Libera, *Introduction à la mystique rhénane,
d'Albert* à Maitre Eckhart, (Paris, 1984), which brings the research together.

116. In so many ways, Eckhart is an exception. Like the others he
spoke of a conversion to self and source (de Libera, op. cit., p. 261), but
unlike them he thought of a total disappropriation of self, of creatures, and
of God (ib., pp. 57, 244, 248), so that God can come to birth in the soul
(8b., pp. 248-59), in a union whose description as 'identity' brought him
ecclesiastical censure. de Libera suspects a tradition going back to John
Scotus Eriugena (*ib.*, pp. 299 n. 53, 309 n. 147). The latter had sought to
preserve divine transcendence by describing it as 'nothing' (v. W.
Beierwaltes, 'Das Problem des absoluten Selbstbewusstseins bei Johannes
Scotus Eriugena', in *Platonismus in der Philosophie des Mittelalters*, Weg
der Forschung 197, (Darmstadt, 1969), (collected from *Philosophisches
Jahrbuch*, 73 (1965-6)), pp. 496, 514: man may only know that God is, not
what he is (p. 514).)

their speculative mysticism,[117] but they had to develop his thought. Albert wrote of the emanation of intelligibilities, but gave virtually no consideration to their return.

Ulrich of Strasburg brought together Augustinian and pseudo-Dionysian conceptions of a conversion of things to a self-knowing God.[118] Dietrich of Freiberg brought the corresponding theses of Proclus's *Elements* into this conception of conversion.[119] Berthold of Moosburg wrote an enormous commentary on the *Theological Elements*, which he used as a means of interrelating Fathers and philosophers.[120] In the part so far published, Berthold correlates, early in the work, pseudo-Dionysius with Proclus on the ecstatic union of man with the divine, and conceives the whole work on the plan of an outgoing and return to the divine Good.[121] Besides the *Elements*, few Latin translations of Proclus were

117. *Vide*, de Libera, op. cit., pp. 10, 35, 37-41, 53, 55, 88, 358-64, 443-6; also L. Sturlese, 'Albert der Grosse und die deutsche philosophische Kultur des Mittelalters', *Freiburger Zeitschrift für Philosophie und Theologie*, 28 (1981), pp. 133-47.

118. *Vide*, de Libera, op. cit., pp. 121-4.

119. *Ib.*, pp. 174-6, 185, 193-99.

120. *Cf.* ib., pp. 338-9: he regarded the *Elements* 'as a true, living organism, capable of assimilating, integrating, filtering all the texts and all the teachings of tradition. In relation to his predecessors, Berthold no longer seems to harmonise his sources, which he only observes as they spring and fly out, on their own and in very determined places from the harmonious proclean system. Seen in this perspective, the *Elements* is the source-book, if you like, the book which contains the whole.' On the MSS (only two remain) and the significance of the work, v. also Boese, op. cit., pp. 69-83.

121. *Vide*, Barbara de Mottoni Faes, 'Il Commento di Bertold di Moosburg all' "Elementatio Theologica" de Proçlo', *Studi Medievali*, 3rd series, XII (1971), pp. 425-6 n. 51, and pp. 423-4 n. 46. The work is set in a

available.[122] Though these thinkers were interested above all in noetic, being was for them not so much transformed into thought as its correlative.[123] From a renewed interest in neo-Platonist texts, Nicholas of Cusa later conceived of God with a single 'vision' of Himself and his creation; but the philosopher's own self-knowledge is not engaged as he regards the Creator with religious awe.[124]

The preoccupation of these German thinkers with noetic and self-knowing, and the neo-Platonist element in their thought, has raised the question of whether there is a connection between them and the later German philoso-

mystical perspective: 'deinde quaerit eorum causas si quomodo ad eas possit pervenire principaliter atque incommutabiliter manentes in Verbo Dei' (Prologue, Vat. Lat. 2192 (I), fo. lrb). de Libera discusses the 'scientific' significance of his image of a mirror reflecting light back to its source, instead of the usual model of a circle, for conversion (op. cit., pp. 419-23). A full appreciation awaits the publication of the complete text (362 folios in Vat. Lat. 2192 !) by Sr. and Sra. Sturlese (in *Temi e Testi*: only the last part has appeared (18 (1974)).

122. Besides three opuscules and the commentary on the *Parmenides* (rarely cited), a partial transl. of his *Timaeus* commentary (v. G. Verbeke, 'Guillaume de Moerbeke, Traducteur de Proclus', *Revue Philosophique de Louvain*, 51 (1953), pp. 349-73). For utilisation, v. de Libera, op. cit., pp. 30-33. For diffusion, v. L. Sturlese, 'Proclo ed Ermete in Germania di Alberto Magno a Bertold di Moosburg. Per una prospettiva di Ricerca sulla cultura filosofica tedesca nel canto delle sue origini (1250-1350)', in *Von Meister Dietrich zu Meister Eckhart*, ed. K. Flasch. Corpus Philosophorum Teutonicorum Medii Aevi, Beiheft 2 (Hamburg, 1984).

123. *Cf.* de Libera, op. cit., p. 167: 'the interlacing of knowing and being is the characteristic of Rhineland thought'.

124. So much emerges from W. Beierwaltes, 'Visio Absoluta, Reflexion als Grundzug des göttlichen Prinzips bei Nicolaus Cusanus', *Sitzungberichte der Heidelberger Akademie der Wissenschaften*, Philosoph.-historische Klasse, 1978, Abhandlung 1. Nicholas had read Berthold's commentary: v. Boese, op. cit., p. 70.

phers from Kant.[125] Any tradition was severely interrupted, and their preoccupations are diverse. Yet Hegel's earliest biographer states how, early in his career, he copied out passages of Tauler and Eckhart 'from literary periodicals';[126] and he once cites Eckhart: 'The eye with which God sees me

125. B. Mojsisch, in *Die Theorie des Intellects bei Dietrich von Freiberg*, Beiheft 1 to *Dietrich von Freiberg Omnia Opera*, (Hamburg, 1977), pp. 12-3, relates his theory to the spontaneity in Fichte's and Kant's conceptions. K. Flasch, in 'Zum Ursprung der neutzeitlichen Philosophie im Späten Mittelalter', *Philosophisches Jahrbuch*, 85 (1978), pp. 1-18, is principally concerned with Dietrich. He is concerned in particular with self-knowing, or self-presence, as productive of being (for which cf. de Libera, op. cit., pp. 168, 184, 198). But even though Dietrich's 'self-consciousness of an all containing reason (Vernunft) . . . comes near to transcendental philosophy' (p. 18), not too much expectancy should be aroused by it. At the heart of Plotinus's system, the conversion of self-thinking Mind and Soul to themselves and their source was productive (the former of Soul, the latter of the material world). Such transcendentalism Hegel found in neo-Platonism, and he found it complete, the end of a particular development. But Hegel went on to propose the sublimation of the difference of pure mind and reality into the absolute idea. cf. Booth, 'A Confrontation', pp. 72-3; also 'Hegel and the Intellectuality of the Fathers', to appear in *Studia Patristica* (Oxford Congress of 1983). v. also the references in de Libera, op. cit., p. 209, n. 3, and author references in his bibliography.

126. K. Rosenkranz, *Hegels ursprüngliches System, 1798 — 1806*, found in *Literarhistorisches Taschebuch*, ed. R.E. Prutz, 2 (1844), pp. 153-242, v. p. 161 (an extract from which is in Hegel, *Werke*, vol. 2 (Frankfurt am Main, 1972), p. 536): 'Among Hegel's papers, as early as the beginning of his period in Switzerland, are to be found extracts of passages from Meister Eckhart and Tauler, which he copied from literary periodicals (Literaturzeitungen).' But this does not coincide with the witness of Baader. v. T.F. O'Meara, O.P., *Romantic Idealism and Roman Catholicism, Schelling and the Theologians*, (Notre Dame and London, 1982), p. 89: (after 1812) 'Once I read (to Hegel) from the works of Meister Eckhart, whom he knew only by name . . . and at the end (he) said, ''There we have it, just what we wanted.'

is the eye with which I see him; my eye and his are one'.[127]

Early in this lecture I mentioned how both Augustine and Descartes had found a safeguard against total scepticism in the certainty of '*cogito* (or *dubito*) *ergo sum*'. But Descartes' own distinction between extended or material, substance, and thinking substance, contributed to a crisis of uncertainty about the reality outside of thinking substance, of which the ultimate stocktaking was in the three *Critiques* of Immanuel Kant.

According to the first critique (of pure reason), the real self is as undiscernable as any other real object. Kant distinguished between the understanding (*Verstand*) which spontaneously brought sense knowledge into order through rules[128], and the reason (*Vernunft*) which was a source of principles and brought order into the intellect's rules, since it's own concepts contain the unconditioned which is not precisely experienced.[129] 'Reason never applies itself directly to experience or to any object';[130] for 'the pure reason is in fact occupied with nothing but itself, and can have no other

127. Quoted in *Vorlesungen über die Philosophie der Religion* I, *SW* (cf. n. 8) 15, p. 228. cf. E. Lichtenstein, 'Von Meister Eckhart bis Hegel, zur philosophische Entwicklung des deutschen Bildungsbegriffs in *Kritik und Metaphysik, Heinz Heimsoeth zum 80 Geburtstag*, (Berlin, 1966), pp. 260-98: it is a study of a *series* of conceptions of *Bildung*, making a link between platonism and (eighteenth century) Lutheran pietism (p. 272).

128. *Kritik der reinen Vernunft* (= $K_r V$: A first edn.; B second edn.), A pp. 50-2; B pp. 74-6. (Standard English transl. by N. Kemp Smith.)

129. *Ib.*, A pp. 298-302, B pp. 355-9; A p. 311, B p. 367.

130. *Ib.*, A p. 302, B p. 359.

task.'[131] The purpose of this critique is to discern reason's attempts to apply to empirical experience principles which are abstract and unreal.[132] Hence it analyses sensible experience of phenomena, and sets out the conditions under which it takes place. Even though the understanding combines sense impressions together with a common relationship to an 'I think',[133] this gives no more than the knowledge that 'I am'.[134] There are impressions of the self as there are impressions of other objects, but these reveal just as little: 'I have no knowledge of myself as I am but only as I appear to myself: the consciousness of self is thus very far from being a knowledge of the self.'[135] The conceptions of a self that is substantial, simple or even continuous are an unjustified imposition of the schemata which reason contains in itself.[136]

131. *Ib.*, A p. 680, B p. 708. An expression at once of reason's dignity, and its total remoteness; reminiscent of the self-thinking of Aristotle's *Metaphysics* XII, 9, but not devine; in its practical use, able to be free from the necessity within its own nature, but in that use not a *coordinator* of the other powers.

132. *Ib.*, Preface to A, pp. vi-viii.

133. *Ib.*, B p. 137: 'without such combinations nothing can be thought or known, since the given representations would not have in common the act of the apperception 'I think', and so could not be apprehended together in one self-consciousness.'

134. *Ib.*, B p. 157: 'in the synthetic original unity of apperception, I am conscious of myself, not as I appear to myself, nor as I am in myself, but only that I am.'

135. *Ib.*, B p. 158.

136. This is demonstrated in the 'paralogisms' of pure reason: a pp. 341-405, with a briefer version in B pp. 406-32. (The latter virtually unites the self as thinking and determining with the noumental (= real) self.) cf. summary at A pp. 682-4, B pp. 710-12.

So searching is his critique of pure reason that it gives an impression of almost complete scepticism. However, the second and third critiques make it clear that he does accept the existence of an objective, intelligible world,[137] and that rational beings have at the same time a sensuous existence under empirically conditioned laws, and a suprasensuous existence under the autonomy of pure reason.[138] But no speculative object can occupy the ultimate place in this world;

137. Evident in the conception of 'noumena', in the first critique. The second critique (of practical reason) speaks of the moral law transferring us into 'an intelligible order of things': the pure reason had established the concept of noumena, but could give no definite knowledge of them: *Kritik der praktischen Vernunft*, ($= K_3V$) 1st edn.: A, p. 73. (Standard English transl. by L.W. Beck.) The third critique (of judgment) speaks of the suprasensuous (Übersinnliche) 'which we have to place under nature as phenomena'; 'the suprasensuous substrate (Substrat) . . . of which we know nothing': *Kritik der Urteilskraft*, Ø78, 1st edn. A, pp. 354 and 357-8, 2nd edn. B pp. 358 and 362. It would be surprising if Kant were more than agnostic to the intelligible substrates of the proclean tradition: v. supra, at n. 90.

138. *Vide*, *KpR*, A pp. 74-5: 'The sensuous nature of rational beings in general is their existence under empirically conditioned laws, and therefore it is, from the point of view of reason, heteronomy. The suprasensuous nature of the same beings, on the other hand, is their existence according to laws which are independent of all empirical conditions and which therefore belong to the autonomy of pure reason. And since the laws, according to which the existence of things depends on cognition, are practical, suprasensuous nature, so far as we can form a concept of it, is nothing else than nature under the autonomy of pure practical reason. The law of this autonomy is the moral law, and it, therefore, is the fundamental law of suprasensuous nature and of a pure world of the understanding, whose counterpart must exist in the world of sense without interfering with the laws of the latter. The former could be called the archetypal world (*natura archetypa*) which we know only by reason; the latter, on the other hand, could be called the ectypal world (*natura ectypa*), because it contains the possible effect of the idea of the former as the determining ground of the will.'

that is given to reason in its practical employment, in the exercise of a sovereign freedom independently of the laws of nature which together make up an unfree mechanism.[139] Acting freely and spontaneously according to the moral law, which it has itself given, a complete structure of subjectivity is disclosed, in which the person, whilst belonging to the intelligible world, can subject that part of himself in the sensible world, to himself.[140] Hence, practical reason could guarantee the conceptions of simple substantiality and duration to the soul, which the speculative reason could not;[141]

139. *KpR*, A, pp. 83-4: 'I leave to the mechanism of natural necessity the right to ascend from conditioned to condition *ad infinitum*, while on the other hand, I hold open for speculative reason the place which for it is vacant, i.e. the intelligible, in order to put the unconditioned in it. I could not, however, give content to this supposition, i.e. convert it into knowledge even of the possibility of a being acting in this way. Pure practical reason now fills this vacant place with a definite law of causality in an intelligible world (causality through freedom). This is the moral law.'

140. KpR, A, p. 155: 'personality, i.e. the freedom and independence from the mechanism of the whole of nature regarded as a capacity of a being which is subject to special laws (pure practical laws given by its own reason), so that the person belonging to the world of sense is subject to his own personality so far as he belongs to the intelligible world.'

141. *KpR*, A, p. 239: 'It leads . . . to the problem of immortality, in the solution of which speculative reason could only commit paralogisms, because the marks of permanence, by which the psychological concept of an ultimate subject necessarily ascribed to the soul in self-consciousness, were lacking though they were needed to complete the real conception of substance. Practical reason, through the postulates of fitness to the moral law in the highest good as the whole end of practical reason, consigns to this subject the requisite duration.' cf. conclusion of critique: id. A, pp. 288-9: ' . . . the starry heavens above me and the moral law within me . . . : I see them before me and I associate them directly with the consciousness of my own existence. . . . (The moral law) begins at my invisible self, my personality, and exhibits me in a world which has true infinity.'

but at the cost of abandoning any transcendence for the limitations of immanence.[142]

In order to remove the distinction between the sensuous and suprasensuous elements of the self in the theoretical use of reason, Fichte proposed a completely subjectivist reinterpretation of Kant. He conceived of the self — the 'I': 'Ich' — as 'positing' itself through itself.[143] Only this self-positing has significant reality. 'The question may well be asked: *what* was I before I arrived at self-consciousness? To which the natural answer is: *I* was nothing at all, since I was not I. The I exists in so far, and to the extent that, it is conscious of itself.'[144] This I may be generalisable for humanity, but it still remains the I of each individual. It seeks to extend itself beyond its limitations, to find liberty. It confronts what is not itself, the not-I (which includes even the

142. *Id.*, A, p. 83: 'Thus reason, which with its ideas always became transcendent when proceding in a speculative manner, can be given for the first time an objective, although still only practical, reality; its transcendent use is changed into an immanent use, whereby reason becomes, in the field of experience, an efficient cause through ideas.'

143. *Vide*, *Grundlage der Gesammten Wissenschaftlehre*, 2nd edn. of 1802, in *Fichtes Sämmtliche Werke*, ed. I.H. Fichte (8 vols, Berlin, 1845-6; photographically reprinted, Berlin, 1971), vol. 1 (both versions), pp. 96-7 (page references to this edition in margins of the *Gesamtausgabe*, of the Bayerische Akademie der Wissenschaften, I,2 (Stuttgart — Bad Canstatt, 1965); publication of series began 1962; still in progress). 'The I posits itself and it is . . . . It is at the same time the one doing and what is produced from the doing; the one that acts, and the product of the acting; doing and acting are one and the same; and so the 'I am' is an expression of an activity-being-done (Thathandlung) . . . . The possibility of (the question, whether this posited I is distinguished from a substrate of consciousness) arises from an uncertainty involving the I as subject and the I as object of the reflexion of the absolute subject . . . . Without noticing, one thinks the absolute subject *in addition* (mit hinzu), while looking at that substrate.'

144. *Ib.*, p. 97. Note the variation: '*i*ch war nicht *I*ch'.

39

inactive element in itself[145]), and transforms it into itself: 'as such the not-I has in itself no reality; but it has reality in so far as it is passive to the I'.[146]

Fichte expressed the basis of his philosophy as the equality of the I with itself: $I = I$; that is, the I has a constitutional need to coincide with itself. Augustine had found that, not only was there a 'perfect and equal' likeness between self-knowing and self-known in the act of self-knowing,[147] but that this equalityconstituted the basic structure of mind.[148] For Fichte the equality of the conscious I with itself was specifically not to be *brought into* consciousness, but to be created, or posited, in the I, whose self-equality would become apparent. For Augustine the equality in the self-knowledge of the thinking I had always existed, but had to be brought into consciousness; and it was the condition of all other knowing.

For the young Schelling and Hegel, Fichte's position on the function and vitality of the I was a call to freedom, and the promise of a renewal of philosophy. In this mood Schelling wrote in *On the I as Principle of Philosophy*, that 'the whole task of theoretical and practical philosophy is nothing than the solution of the contradictions between the pure

145. *Ib.*, p. 138: 'The I is *only* active; it is pure I in so far as it is active; and in so far as it is not active it is not-I.'

146. *Ib.*, p. 135.

147. *De Trinitate*, IX 11,16: 'completely matching and equal, and continually so' (par omnino et aequale atque identidem); 'a perfect and equal likeness by which the mind itself which knows is known.'

148. *Vide, ib.*, IX 11.18, cited in n. 69, supra. In including self-memory, Augustine gave an ennead of mutual equalities.

and empirically conditioned I.'[149]

However, with Schelling disenchantment soon set in; for Fichte's position did not adequately account for the reality outside the I. He experimented with a figure in which a philosophy of nature was identical with a philosophy of the I, each demanding the other, but with nature falling short. To Hegel, Fichte and Schelling were proposing a union of subject and object which would end the dualism found in the philosophies of Descartes and Kant,[150] but neither had succeeded. Fichte had established no more than a subjective subject-object, whilst Schelling had established no more than an objective subject-object.[151]

Hegel constructed another philosophy of subject-object, in which their union, through the penetration of object by subject and transformation into itself, was progressively effected by self-consciousness which had become reason.[152] Hegel proposed that nature had gone forth from mind, and was returning into union with it. His language is precisely that of neo-Platonist conversion; but the significance is different: one factor in the single divine Idea externalises itself, and, in its returning into a profounder union in

149. *Vom Ich als Princip der Philosophie, oder über das Unbedingte im menschlichen Wissen*, (1st edn, 1795), in *Sämtliche Werke*, abth.1, bd. 1, (Stuttgart, etc., 1861), p. 176.

150. *Vide*, texts collected in Booth, 'A Confrontation', p. 62.

151. *Vide*, Introduction to *Differenz des Fichte'schen und Schelling'schen Systems der Philosophie*, SW (cf. n. 8 supra), vol. 1, pp. 33-8. On the contrary he said, subject and object were sublimated to identity in the Absolute (*ib.*, pp. 123-4); the force behind this sublimation is the 'secret efficacy of reason', *ib.*, p. 51.

152. *Phänomenologie des Geistes*, *SW* 2, p. 183: 'Now that self-consciousness is reason . . . it is certain that it is itself reality, and that everything actual is none other than itself.'

diversity with the other, is the foundation of self-consciousness.[153] With Schelling, Hegel had early discovered the relevance of the neo-Platonists' thought to their own.[154] His system has all the simplicity of Plotinus's account of the mind's return to itself, which Proclus had rejected,[155] and yet in its dialectical articulation a resemblance to Proclus's mediating hierarchies. But he explicitly says that the one-sidedness of Neo-platonist transcendence has to be surpassed in a union of thought and reality, the true subject-object. Before this process is complete in the absolute idea, the idea first develops itself as logical, as 'enveloped in pure thought';[156] this is in the passage from pure undifferentiated being[157] to the concept: the idea of a thing in a self-conscious mind, able to absorb the thing into itself, having always been its model and its truth. Self-conscious mind — the mind of the philosopher in the act of philosophising — sinks itself into the object, coincides with the object's movement, and takes it into itself as the other side

153. *System der Philosophie* (= *Enzyklopädie*) II, Ø 247z, *SW* 9, p. 49: 'The divine idea is just this: to disclose itself, to posit this other outside itself, and to take it back again into itself, in order to be subjectivity and Geist. The philosophy of nature itself belongs to this path of return.'

154. *Vide*, Booth, 'A Confrontation', pp. 70-75. In the history of philosophy, neo-platonism was a complete development, but one-sided; it showed thought in the process of returning to itself, but not the absolute unity of concept with objectivity.

155. *Vide*, supra, at nn. 82-4.

156. *Wissenschaft der Logik* II, *SW* 5, p. 352. Marx wrongly supposed that the logical idea was equivalent to the absolute idea: v. infra at n. 172.

157. Which is therefore 'Nichts'. Perhaps this arises from Kant's saying that 'being' is not a real predicate, and that logically it is merely the copula in a judgement: $K_r V$, A p. 598, B p. 626.

42

of a single subject-object.[158] In this way, self-consciousness recognises 'that in its certainty of itself it is all reality'.[159] Following out its movement of conversion,[160] self-conscious mind develops a progressive order of categories — a logic — by which it may unite external reality to itself, to make it 'true reality' (*Wirklichkeit*); it turns to nature to reunite that with itself, and then to within itself to fathom its own reality, and eventually to construct a political state from the union of self-conscious individuals. Logic, the philosophy of nature, the philosophy of mind, as a triad of sciences, all raised to self-conscious existence in the philosopher's mind come together, on the model of Proclus's intelligible Gods,[161] in a triad of triads at the end of the *Encyclopedia*, with each one predominating in turn, but ending with the Idea of philosophy — the Idea articulated in logic, recognising nature and mind as its manifestations, and bringing them into unity. It itself caused their development, and it itself recognises — in full-self-consciousness — itself in

158. *Cf. Phänomenologie, SW* 2, pp. 50-1: 'scientific knowledge' (i.e. that of the philosopher) 'requires more the passage into the life of the object. . . . Being sunk in the material and coinciding with its movement, it comes back to itself, but not before it takes its completeness into itself, simplified to being a determination, reduced to being one side of an existent entity, and passes into its higher truth.' v. Booth, 'A Confrontation', p. 84. Also, cf. *id.*, p. 612: 'self-consciousness enriches itself till it has wrested from consciousness the entire substance and has absorbed the entire structure of the essentialities of substance. . . . it has produced them out of itself, and in so doing has, at the same time restored them for consciousness.'

159. *Id., SW* 2, p. 183. v. text at n. 152 supra.

160. What follows a brief outline of *System der Philosophie* (= *Enzyklopädie*).

161. *Cf.* supra, at nn. 71-5.

them. And this is 'the eternal Idea', which, 'in full fruition of its essence, eternally sets itself to work, engenders and enjoys itself as absolute mind.'[162] On the way to that climax, Hegel claims that the Christian Trinity expressed the Idea, still in its form of pure thought;[163] for in it the Father has self-consciousness of Himself in the Son, the self-consciousness of the Son is at the same time knowledge of the Father, and the return of love, abolishing the difference between them, is Spirit.[164]

The fact of so much self-thinking in Hegel's system led Schelling to exclaim: 'to be under this necessity of always to be self-thinking is an enormous restriction; no mortal would want to undertake it. Always to be only thinking of oneself must be the most painful condition for any healthy nature.'[165] As also to make his fundamental criticism of Hegel: 'In this unity (of being and thought) the priority is not on the

---

162. *System* III, Ø 577, *SW* 10, p. 475.

163. *Philosophie der Religion* II, *SW* 16, p. 228.

164. Putting together *id*. I, *SW* 15, p. 468, and *id*. II, *SW* 16, p. 308. Though sometimes Spirit is the whole process of positing divisions and cancelling them: 'God is the beginning . . . (and) equally only the end, the totality, and it is a totality that God is Spirit, id. In *System* III, Ø 567, the limitation of the universal Father is begetting the Son, making up concrete individuality, is like the union of finite and infinite in the 'mixed' of Proclus's intelligibles (*SW* 10, p. 455; cf. supra at n. 85). In brief, Hegel's theory of the Trinity sees its components as functions in his conception of mind.

165. From Schelling's lectures on the philosophy of revelation (1841-2), as pirated by Paulus (= Paulus Nachschrift): H.E.G. Paulus, *Die endlich offenbar gewordene positive Philosophie der Offenbarung . . . der v. Schellingischen Entdeckungen über Philosophie überhaupt . . . .* (Darmstadt, 1843), p. 476.(Suhrkamp edn.: F.W.J. Schelling, *Philosophie der Offenbarung 1841/42*), (Frankfurt am Main, 1977), p. 176.

44

side of thought; being is first, thinking comes second as a consequence.'[166]

Is it possible to find in Marx and Engels a continuation of the same theme? In that case the western tradition of self-knowing would unite all of its significant areas of thought, marking out a cultural ecumene. Appearing first as the essence of thought in Aristotle; becoming the key-stone of pagan philosophical syncretism in neo-Platonism; critically adopted by Augustine for the light it could throw on the Christian Godhead and the structure of the human mind; passing in different forms into mediaeval thought; picked up again in Fichte's reworking of Kant's critical philosophy; and so passing to Schelling and Hegel, who soon rediscovered in neo-Platonism themes near to their own; and then did it pass into the anti-mind, anti-philosophy thought of the founders of materialistic communism?

One very informed critic of Marxism seems to make this link, and he gives Marx's dialectic a pre-history back to Plotinus.[167] He writes: 'Marxism . . . is identical with the self-knowledge of the working class; that class comprehends the social process in the very act of revolutionising the world, so that in this one privileged case the understanding

166. *Abhandlung über die Quelle der ewigen Wahrheiten*, *Sämmtliche Werke*, abth. II bd 1, p. 587.
167. *Vide*, L. Kolakowski, *Main Currents of Marxism*, 3 vols. (Oxford, 1978), vol. 1, ch. 1.

and the making of history appear as a single act.'[168]

But from the texts of Marx and Engels themselves, it is clear that they regarded Hegel's conception of self-consciousness with consistent mockery. 'The essence of this self-consciousness is not man but the Idea, whose real existence it is';[169] 'The real subject remains just as before outside the (philosopher's) head, in its independence; just as long as the head takes only a speculative or theoretical attitude.'[170] Marx thought that when Hegel made man and the whole of nature a product (an alienation) of self-conscious mind, he meant that the whole of nature was an abstraction without reality.[171] Marx, and Engels with him, misunderstood Hegel because they thought that he always wrote of the Idea as Absolute idea; he did not understand that when Hegel spoke of the 'pure' idea, he indicated it at its first stage of only logical development. Hence he could not see that it would

168. *Ib.*, vol. 2, pp. 374-5. cf. also the author's comment on Marx's 11th thesis against Feuerbach ('the philosophers have only interpreted the world in various ways; the point however is to change it'): 'it means society understanding itself, an act in which the subject changes the object by the very fact of understanding it. That can only come about when subject and object coincide, when the differences between educator and educated disappear, and when thought becomes a revolutionary act, the self-recognition of human existence': id. vol. 1, p. 144.

169. K. Marx and F. Engels, *Die heilige Familie*, in Karl Marx, Friedrich Engels, *Werke*, 39 vols, 1 Ergänzungsband (2 parts), and Index (Berlin, 1960-83), vol. 2, p. 146.

170. Marx, *Einleitung zur Kritik der Politischen Ökonomie*, *Werke* vol. 13, p. 633.

171. *Vide*, Marx, *Kritik der Hegelschen Dialektik und Philosophie Überhaupt* (in Ökonomisch-philosophische Manuskript (1844)), *Werke* Erganz.bd. I, p. 577: 'it is clear that a self-consciousness through an alienation can only produce thinghood (Dingheit), that is only an abstract thing, a thing produced by abstraction and no real thing.'

46

continue to develop into a union of concept and reality.[172] Similarly, he also assumed that when Hegel wrote of self-consciousness he always meant 'pure self-consciousness.'[173] This is clear from interpretations of Hegel's texts in Marx's writings. Whilst we could suppose that the end of alienation entailed the emergence of an authentic self-consciousness,

172. *Vide*, his interpretation of a text in *System* I (= Logik) Ø 244 (*SW* 8, p. 451): 'The idea, which is for itself, when viewed on the point of this unity with itself, is intuition'. He gratuitously interprets 'idea' here as 'the absolute idea', and does not complete the quotation: 'and the intuited idea (is) nature' (which shows the incompleteness of the idea in 'unity with itself') (v. *Kritik der hegelschen Dialektik*, p. 585). But this is quite incorrect. To use Hegel's own words from a comparable place in the *Wissenchaft der Logik*, 'the idea still is logical, it is enveloped in pure thought, and is the science only of the divine notion': *SW* 5, p. 352.

173. *Vide*, the comments on a passage from the *Wissenschaft de Logik* (*SW* 5, pp. 13-14): 'The concept . . . developing into free existence . . . is nothing other than the I or pure self-consciousness', in *Der heilige Familie*, p. 146. The passage is interpreted on the wrong assumption that self-consciousness in Hegel is always 'pure', just as it was assumed, in the passage quoted in n. 172, that the 'idea' is always 'the absolute idea'. But from what follows it is quite clear that this self-consciousness is not yet complete, and is going on to unite itself with reality: 'When a notion is formed of (the object) . . . the I penetrates it in and by thinking. . . . Hence the object has this objectivity in the notion, and (the notion) is the unity of self-consciousness in which (the object) has been taken up' (*ib.*, p. 16). 'It must indeed be admitted that the notion as such is not yet complete, but must rise into the idea, which is the unity of notion and reality' (*ib.*, p. 19). Yet, it is possible that here is a fickle, if heavy, polemical materialism, for there are texts which indicate an awareness of Hegel's conception of the unity of concept, or thought, or universal, with reality: v. *Die heilige Familie*, p. 145, 'We leave "the universality which reaches a determination", the "singularity and infinity" — of the hegelian concept, to its fate'; *ib.*, p. 147: 'In Hegel are three elements, Spinozistic substance, Fichtean self-consciousness, the hegelian necessarily fully contradictory unity of both, absolute Spirit'; Engels, *Ludwig Feuerbach und der Ausgang der klassische deutsche Philosophie, Werke*, 21, p. 275: 'the identity of thinking and being is 'agreed to by far the greater number of philosophers,' and naturally by Hegel.

Marx and Engels so disparaged the philosophers' conception of self-consciousness as something spun out of the head or brain, that one must conceive of the proletariat as having a self-consciousness in the revolutionary act which would find no parallel in the theme which I have presented. According to Engels, whilst dialectic according to Hegel is the 'self-development of thinking', its real nature 'in our head' is a reflection of the dialectic, complete in itself, in the world of nature and human history.[174] Human nature has, therefore, no bedrock in thinking and self-thinking, and consciousness develops in function of the mechanisms of nature, for a self that might desire development, but is assuredly not free. Augustine's conception of the place of self-knowing in human subjectivity shows why this conception is so far from that of the Christian culture.

The relation of Augustine's conception of self-knowing to Hegel's has been treated elsewhere,[175] and the conclusion was drawn that, from Hegel's point of view, the self-consciousness of Augustine 'would not really have begun to possess itself'.[176] Hegel's self-consciousness is not something posited, as in Fichte; it is more like Augustine's as

174. In correspondence: *Werke*, vol. 38, p. 204: 'the dialectic in our head is only the reflection of the factual development fulfilled in the world of nature and human history, obeying the dialectical forms.' In rejecting thinking and self-thinking, Marx's thought, not surprisingly, finds itself as the other metaphysical polarity of being: 'not only in thinking, in consciousness, but in wholesale being (in massenhaften Sein)', *Die heilige Familie*, p. 56.

175. *Vide*, Booth, 'Hegel's Conception of Self-Knowledge, Seen in Conjunction with Augustine's', *Augustiniana*, 30 (1980), pp. 221-250.

176. *Ib.*, p. 232; cf. p. 230, and n. 44, pp. 249-50.

'man's genuine reality'.[177] But while that core of self-knowing in Augustine, as the condition of knowing everything else, is revealed in a process of self-discovery, it is not destined to become the knowledge, still less the reality, of everything else; and this reticence indicates an ease with oneself, and thereby a truer shape of subjectivity, which a theoretically possible, total self-possession would discompose.

Augustine's call to interiority reaches to ears and hearts where the philosophers' often obscure expressions have no entrance. For, as with Kant, though in a way which extends beyond the philosophical, moral factors come into this metaphysical question. Of what use is a man to himself, if he is not sure that, in his depths, he is built on self-certainty? Of what use is a man to others, if he first of all does not know himself? Of what value is a society united only by extrinsic goals, and in imitating extrinsic models, and which has thereby forgotten its depths? Or a society in which an inner certainty of self must be broken down, brutally if needs be, to receive a new self, said to be the product of natural processes?

With a simple and easily memorable structure, Augustine encourages every man to find, within the unattainable totality of himself, the wholeness of himself as knower, always equal to the wholeness of himself as known. Not now as an archaic restoration, or as an abruptly re-conceived remedy, but as the inevitable concomitant of the human nature of whatever age; for, unlike being, that other great metaphysical polarity, self-knowing has to have a continuing, unceasing history.

177. *System* III, § 377, *SW* 10, p.9.

THE SAINT AUGUSTINE LECTURES

1959   *Saint Augustine on Personality*, by Paul Henry, S.J., Institut Catholique, Paris; New York, The Macmillan Company, 1960.

1960   *Platonism and Augustinianism*, by Raymond Klibansky, McGill University; unpublished.

1961   *Charter of Christendom: the Significance of the City of God*, by John O'Meara, University College, Dublin; New York, The Macmillan Company, 1961.

1962   *At the Origins of the Thomistic Notion of Man*, by Anton Pegis, Pontifical Institute of Mediaeval Studies, Toronto; New York, The Macmillan Company, 1963.

1963   *Augustine's View of Reality*, by Vernon J. Bourke, St. Louis University; Villanova, Villanova Press, 1964.

1964   *Augustine and the Greek Philosophers*, by John F. Callahan, Georgetown University; Villanova, Villanova University Press, 1967.

1965   *The Resurrection and Saint Augustine's Theology of Human Values*, by Henri I. Marrou, University of Paris; Villanova, Villanova University Press, 1966.

1966   *St. Augustine and Christian Platonism*, by A. Hilary Armstrong, University of Liverpool; Villanova, Villanova University Press, 1967.

1967   *Saint Augustine on Creation*, by Paul Henry, S.J., Institut Catholique; Paris, University of California, San Diego; unpublished.

1968   *Augustine on Immortality*, by John A. Mourant, The Pennsylvania State University, University Park, Pa.; Villanova, Villanova University Press, 1969.

1969   *Augustinian Personalism*, by Mary T. Clark, R.S.C.J., Manhattanville College, Post-Doctoral Fellow, Yale University; Villanova, Villanova University Press, 1970.

1970   *Augustine and Modern Research on Pelagianism*, by Gerald Bonner, Durham University, England; Villanova, Villanova University Press, 1972.

1971   *Political Idealism and Christianity in the Thought of St. Augustine*, by Ernest L. Fortin, Boston College; Villanova, Villanova University Press, 1972.

1972   *Saint Augustin et la dialectique*, by Jean Pépin, École Pratique des Hautes Études, Paris; Villanova, Villanova University Press, 1976.

1973   *Augustine's Strategy as an Apologist*, by Eugene TeSelle, Vanderbilt University, Nashville, Tennessee; Villanova, Villanova University Press, 1974.

1974   *Church, State and Toleration: An Intriguing Change of Mind in Augustine*, by Emilien Lamirande, University of Ottawa, Ottawa, Canada; Villanova, Villanova University Press, 1975.

1975   *St. Augustine's Monasticism in the Light of Acts 4.32-35*, by Luc Verheijen, O.S.A., École Pratique des Hautes Études, Paris: Villanova, Villanova University Press, 1979.

1976   *The Confessions of St. Augustine: A Reappraisal*, by Alberto Pincherle, Professor Emeritus, University of Rome, printed in Volume 7, *Augustinian Studies*; Villanova, Augustinian Institute, 1976.

1977   *The Creation of Man in St. Augustine's De Genesi ad Litteram*, by John J. O'Meara, University College, Dublin; Villanova, Villanova University Press, in press.

1978   *Joy in Augustine's Ethics*, by Vernon J. Bourke, Professor Emeritus, St. Louis University; Villanova, Villanova University Press, 1979.

1979   *St. Augustine on Memory*, by John A. Mourant, Professor Emeritus, The Pennsylvania State University, University Park, Pa.; Villanova, Villanova University Press, 1980.

1980   Regio Beatitudinis. *Augustine's Concept of Happiness*, by Werner Beierwaltes, Albert Ludwigs Universität, Freiburg; Villanova, Villanova University Press, 1981.

1981   *Saint Augustine's Platonism*, by Robert J. O'Connell, S.J., Fordham University; Villanova, Villanova University Press, 1984.

1982   *The Conversions of Saint Augustine*, by Leo C. Ferrari, St. Thomas University, Fredericton, N.B., Canada; Villanova, Villanova University Press, 1984.

1983   *Catechesis in St. Augustine*, by Eugene Kevane, Notre Dame Pontifical Catechetical Institute; Villanova, Villanova University Press, in press.

1984   *Conversion and Disenchantment in Augustine's Spiritual Career*, by Robert A. Markus, University of Nottingham; Villanova, Villanova University Press, in press.

1985   *Saint Augustine and the Saints*, by Robert Bryan Eno, S.S., The Catholic University of America; Villanova, Villanova University Press, in press.

Publications of:
VILLANOVA UNIVERSITY
AUGUSTINIAN INSTITUTE
Villanova, Pa. 19085-1699

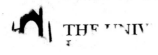THE UNIV